First Facts®

OUR PLACE IN THE UNIVERSE

THE MOON AND OTHER SATELLITES

by Ellen Labrecque

CAPSTONE PRESS
a capstone imprint

First Facts is published by Capstone
1710 Roe Crest Drive, North Mankato, Minnesota 56003
www.mycapstone.com

Library of Congress Cataloging-in-Publication Data
Names: Labrecque, Ellen, author.
Title: The moon and other satellites / by Ellen Labrecque.
Description: North Mankato, Minnesota : an imprint of Pebble, [2020] |
    Series: First facts. Our place in the universe | "Pebble is published by
    Capstone." | Audience: Ages 6-9. | Audience: K to grade 3.
Identifiers: LCCN 2018056096| ISBN 9781977108494 (hardcover) | ISBN
    9781977110190 (pbk.) | ISBN 9781977108661 (ebook pdf)
Subjects: LCSH: Satellites--Juvenile literature. | Moon--Juvenile literature.
Classification: LCC QB401.5 .L33 2020 | DDC 523.3--dc23
LC record available at https://lccn.loc.gov/2018056096

Editorial Credits

Hank Musolf, editor; Kyle Grenz, designer; Jo Miller, media researcher; Kathy McColley, production
specialist

Photo Credits

NASA; JPL-Caltech, 7, W. Liller, 19; Shutterstock: BlueRingMedia, 9, Cristian Cestaro, Cover, Dotted Yeti,
17 (Both), jakkapan, 15, kdshutterman, 5, kdshutterman, 21, Korionov, 22, Nevada31, 11, psoundphoto, 9,
robert_s, 8, Siberian Art, 13
Design Elements
Capstone; Shutterstock: Alex Mit, Dimonika, Kanate

All internet sites appearing in back matter were available and accurate when this book was sent to press.

Printed and bound in China
1671

Table of Contents

Meet the Moons

What is one of the brightest objects in our night sky? The moon! The moon doesn't make its own light. It **reflects** the sun's light.

FAR-OUT FACT

Twelve people have visited our moon. It is the only other space object besides Earth people have stood on.

reflect—to return light from an object; the moon reflects light from the sun

The Earth has one moon.
Other planets have more than one.
Moons are **satellites**. They **orbit** a
planet or a star. Let's learn about
the many moons in our **universe**.

orbit—to travel around an object in space

satellite—an object in space that moves around a planet or a star

universe—everything that exists, including the Earth, the stars, and all of space

Earth's Moon

Our moon formed more than 4 billion years ago. Scientists think it formed when a giant **asteroid** hit the Earth. The big smash sent many bits into space. Over time, the bits formed into the moon.

FAR-OUT FACT

The moon is much smaller than Earth. Fifty moons could fit inside our planet.

asteroid—a rocky object in space

The moon's surface is covered in craters. A crater is a bowl-shaped pit. The craters formed when asteroids slammed into the moon. The moon does not have an **atmosphere** like Earth to protect itself.

atmosphere—gases that surround planets or other objects in space

We only see one side of the
moon from Earth. We call this
side the near side. The other
is called the far side. We never
see this side from Earth.

The moon takes 27 days to orbit the Earth. It spins slowly as it orbits. It spins just once during the 27 days. Earth's gravity keeps the same side of the moon always facing us.

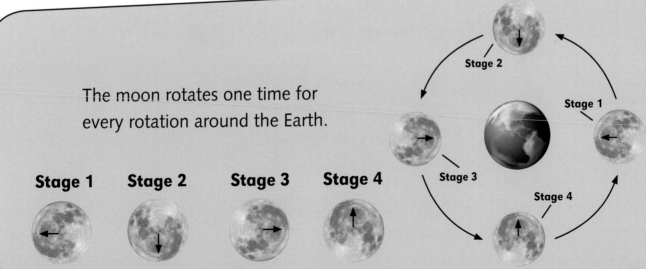

The moon rotates one time for every rotation around the Earth.

Stage 1 **Stage 2** **Stage 3** **Stage 4**

The moon is a giant ball of rock. But from Earth, it looks like different shapes. This is because of the way the sun hits it. Sometimes the sun lights up the whole moon. Other times it lights up just a sliver. Sometimes it hardly lights up any shape at all. These changes are called the phases of the moon.

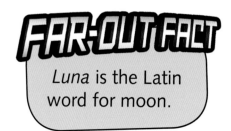

FAR-OUT FACT

Luna is the Latin word for moon.

Phases of the Moon

New Moon

Waxing Crescent

First Quarter

Waxing Gibbous

Full Moon

Waning Gibbous

Last Quarter

Waning Crescent

New Moon

Eclipse

An eclipse happens when one object in space moves in the shadow of another object.

A lunar eclipse is an eclipse of the moon. The Earth moves in between the moon and the sun. The Earth blocks the sunlight that usually is reflected by the moon. This can only happen when we see a full moon from Earth.

Lunar Eclipse

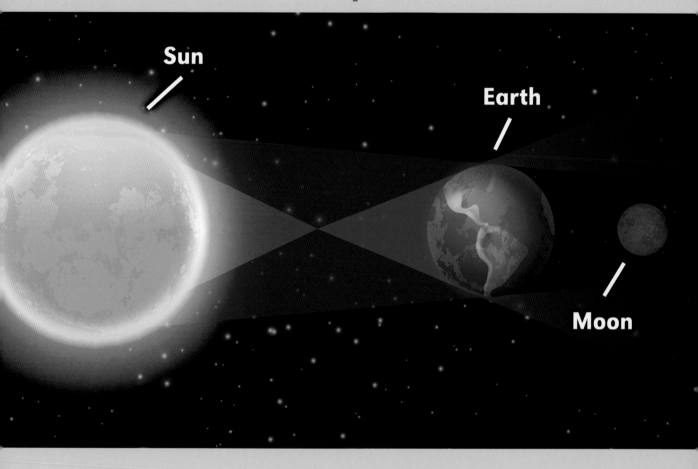

Sun

Earth

Moon

FAR-OUT FACT

A moon must be smaller
than the planet it is orbiting.

The Tide Is High

Did you know the moon changes the ocean's **tides**? When the ocean is at its highest point, it is called a high tide. When it is at its lowest point, it is called a low tide. The rise and fall of the oceans is a result of the moon's pull. We have two low tides and two high tides every day.

tide—the rise or fall of sea level at a certain place

Other Moons

Nobody knows how many moons are in the universe. We know that there are 181 moons in our solar system. Our solar system is made up of the sun and the planets that orbit around it. Earth is one of these planets. The giant planet Jupiter has the most moons. It has 67.

FAR-OUT FACT

The four planets Jupiter, Saturn, Uranus, and Neptune have more than 140 moons between them.

Jupiter and some of its many moons

Active Volcanoes

One of Jupiter's moons is named Io. Io has many active volcanoes on it. Its surface is covered in **lava**. Some of the lava that erupts out of the volcanoes goes many miles high.

lava—the liquid rock that spews from a volcano

Other Satellites

Besides moons, other satellites are in space. Asteroids also orbit other planets and the sun. **Comets** orbit around planets too. The most famous comet is called Halley's Comet. It orbits the sun every 76 years. We last saw Halley's Comet from Earth in 1986. We could next see it in 2061!

comet—an object in space that has dust and gas around it that form a tail

comets speed through outer space

Look Up!

Don't forget to look up when you are outside at night. Is it a full moon? Is it a half moon? Is it only a crescent? Maybe you can't even see it at all.

Space is an amazing place. Today astronauts still visit the moon to study it. Maybe one day you will go to the moon!

21

Glossary

asteroid (AS-tuh-roid)—a rocky object in space

atmosphere (AT-muhs-feer)—gases that surround planets or other objects in space

comet (KOM-it)—an object in space that has dust and gas around it that form a tail

lava (LAH-vuh)—the liquid rock that spews from a volcano

orbit (OR-bit)— to travel around an object in space

reflect (ri-FLEKT)—to return light from an object; the moon reflects light from the sun

satellite (SAT-uh-lite)—an object in space that moves around a planet or a star

tide (tahyd)—the rise or fall of sea level at a certain place

universe (YOO-nuh-vurs)—everything that exists, including the Earth, the stars, and all of space

Read More

Chown, Marcus. *Solar System: A Visual Exploration of the Planets, Moons, and Other Heavenly Bodies That Orbit Our Sun.* New York: Black Dog and Leventhal, 2016.

Laurberg, Marie. *The Moon: From Inner Worlds to Outer Space.* Louisiana: Louisiana Museum of Modern Art, 2018.

Spilsbury, Richard. *Space.* Adventures in STEAM. North Mankato, MN: Capstone Press, 2019.

Internet Sites

NASA Science: Earth's Moon
https://moon.nasa.gov/about/in-depth/

Windows to the Universe: Our Solar System
https://www.windows2universe.org/our_solar_system/solar_system.html

Critical Thinking Questions

- How do phases of the moon occur?

- How do scientists think craters formed on the moon?

- How does the moon affect the ocean?

Index